KAREN LYNN WILLIAMS's children's books include
Galimoto, a Reading Rainbow Featured Book and one of
the *New York Times* Top Ten Books of the Year.
She worked as a Peace Corps volunteer in Malawi –
the setting for *When Africa Was Home*, a *Booklist* Editors' Choice.
Karen also lived and worked in Haiti – the setting for
her highly acclaimed *Circles of Hope*, and has worked
with refugees from around the world.
She currently lives on the Navajo reservation in Chinle, Arizona,
where she writes, and enjoys learning about the Navajo culture and life
in the Southwest. She has four children scattered across the world.

WENDY STONE's passion for Africa began 20 years ago
when she went to Kenya on a photography assignment for the
Rockefeller Foundation. Since then she has covered civil wars,
droughts and famines in Somalia, Sudan and Ethiopia,
working with UN agencies including UNHCR, WFP,
UNICEF and HABITAT. Her recent work includes
photographic exhibitions for the World Agroforestry Centre,
Alliance for a Green Revolution in Africa (AGRA),
Centers for Disease Control and the Ford Foundation.
Wendy has one daughter and lives in New York City and Nairobi.

For the children of Kibera – K.W.

In memory of my late husband David Light,
who shared my love of Africa – W.S.

Beatrice's Dream copyright © Frances Lincoln Limited 2011
Text copyright © Karen Lynn Williams 2011
Illustrations copyright © Wendy Stone 2011

First published in Great Britain and the USA in 2011 by
Frances Lincoln Children's Books, 4 Torriano Mews,
Torriano Avenue, London NW5 2RZ
www.franceslincoln.com

First paperback published in Great Britain in 2012

With thanks to the Kibera Integrated Community Self-Help Programme (KICOSHEP)
and its founder and director Anne Owiti, for all their help. KICOSHEP provides care
and counselling for people in Kibera suffering from HIV/AIDS,
as well as running a youth centre, supporting orphans and organising sports
and social events for young people.

A catalogue record for this book is available from the British Library.

ISBN 978-1-84780-418-1

Set in Cerigo LT

Printed in Shenzhen, Guangdong, China by C&C Offset Printing in November 2012

1 3 5 7 9 8 6 4 2

Beatrice's Dream

A Story of Kibera Slum

Karen Lynn Williams
Photographs by Wendy Stone

F

FRANCES LINCOLN
CHILDREN'S BOOKS

Jambo! My name is Beatrice.

I am thirteen and the youngest in my family.
My father died in a car accident and my mother
died of tuberculosis when I was nine. Since then
I have always worried about being alone and
wondered who will take care of me.

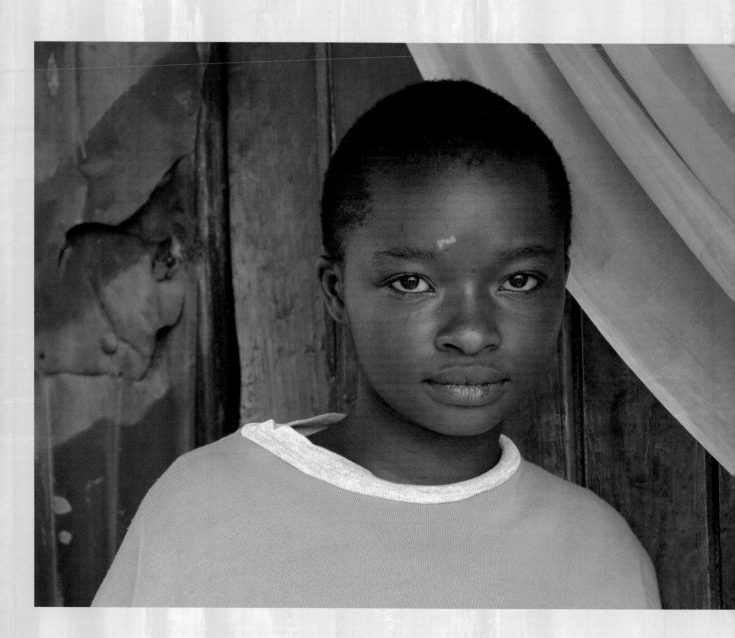

I live in Kibera with Francis, the oldest of my brothers, and his wife. We sleep behind the shop where he sells soap and other small household things.

I am in Class Seven – and I really like my school.

Every morning I put on my uniform and walk to school. It takes me half an hour.

During the rains, no one in Kibera can walk anywhere without getting covered in mud. I wear sandals when it rains, and I have to wash them out every day.

In the dry season there is dust everywhere. It blows in my eyes and between my teeth.

To get to school, I have to cross the railway track
that goes from Mombasa to Kisumu.

Near the railway track you can look out over the slum
and see it stretching on and on to where the earth
meets the sky.

People move around everywhere like ants.
I see them in the market, in the shops, out
playing, working and visiting their friends.

My school is built of tin, and my class is on
the second floor. It is a small room crammed
so full of desks that we can hardly squeeze
past them to get to our seats. When the wind
blows, the loose tin on the roof crackles
and pops. *Ping. Ping.*

Next door, Class Six are singing. On the other side, Class Five are chanting their lessons out loud. It is good to hear so many voices speaking as one.

When my thoughts start to wander and I gaze out of the window, my teacher says, "Beatrice, your body is here, but your spirit is at home."

Kennedy, who sits near me, says, "That is witchcraft!"

My teacher replies, "No – that is daydreaming." Everybody laughs, and the teacher smiles at me.

My favourite subjects are English and Kiswahili, the official language of Kenya. Today I am studying Geometry, learning about triangles and parallel lines. Parallel lines do not meet, even if you follow them right up to heaven!

Sometimes, when I try to guess the answer to a problem, my teacher says, "Stop beating around the bush." She also says, "If a shepherd has a hundred sheep and one gets left behind, that sheep will be eaten by a hyena."

So now I always put up my hand when I don't understand something. I don't want to be eaten by a hyena!

Time for lunch. Today I am the school timekeeper.
I borrow my friend's watch and go outside to ring
the bell ending lessons.

Some of the girls play jump-rope (skipping).
I prefer football and hide-and-seek, but my favourite
game of all is shooting baskets (basketball).

We all wash our hands. For lunch we eat *githeri*,
a special Kenyan dish made from beans and maize.

After lunch, each class takes turns to wash
the plates and serving buckets.

In the afternoon we learn about HIV and AIDS, and about ourselves. Our teacher asks, "What is special about girls?"

We answer, "Girls give birth and nurse children. Girls fetch firewood and water. Girls clean, cook and do the washing."

"But can't boys fetch firewood and clean and cook and do the washing too?" my teacher asks.

Some of us agree with her.

Then she asks, "What can boys do that is special?"

We answer, "They build and repair houses, and provide for their families."

"But can't girls build houses too? Can't they provide for their families too?"

"Yes, they can," we answer.

"Boys and girls must all work together," says my teacher.

I like hearing her say this!

After school we can stay on for extra lessons,
but I have to be home by six o'clock, before
it gets dark. Sometimes my dog, Soldier,
is waiting for me.

At home, I have a wash and help prepare our meal.
Then I iron my clothes.

Later, if we have enough paraffin in our small lamp,
I read. I enjoy reading science and social studies books
most of all.

On Saturdays, I go to school until lunchtime.
We have a small library where we can take off
our shoes, sit on cushions and read.

At our youth centre, some children are putting together books about their families, helped by their grandmothers. I have no one to tell my family's story but the community volunteer says she will help me make a book. She says that lots of people knew my mother, and they will help me remember everything.

. MAHARAGWE
. MAHINDI
. MBAAZI
. MUTHOKOI
. NJAHI

. KUNDE
. SUKARI
. WIMBI PURE
. MAWELE
. MTAMA
. WIMBI MIX
. MIHOGO
. UNGA YA KUPIMA NO.1/2

. NPENGU
. CHAKULA CHA KUKU

G10b
MAKING A WO
OF DIFFE

Back at home, I do the washing and go to market. I'm good at choosing the best value fruit and vegetables. If I have any money left over afterwards, I buy a *chapati*, a thin Indian pancake.

At the weekend I help in my brother's shop, selling small things like matches, sticking plasters and mirrors. I am good at making keys, too, which I choose from a big bundle.

On Monday, the new school week begins. My friend
Gamilla walks there with me.

Today my teacher asks the class, "What do you want
to be when you grow up?"

Some of the students say they want to be teachers
or doctors. I put up my hand. "I want to be a nurse."

Our teacher says that not only boys, but girls too can
be doctors, teachers and nurses!

My dream is to pass my exams, go on to secondary school and study nursing. Then I will help people who are sick or on their own, like me.

Here at school I am not alone, and I feel safe.

My teacher asks, "*Habari gani?* How are you, Beatrice?"

I smile and say, "I am fine."

About Kibera slum

Kibera is in Nairobi, the capital city of Kenya, in east Africa. It is one of the largest slums in sub-Saharan Africa, with over half a million people living there. The slum covers 2.5 square kilometres (618 acres). There are no roads and few of the residents have modern toilets, clean drinking water or electricity. The crime rate is high and disease spreads rapidly.

Many people come to Kibera from rural areas to look for jobs in the city. A large proportion of the children have become orphans because so many adults have died from AIDS – many people in Kibera are infected with the HIV/AIDS virus.

A number of organisations work in the slum offering medical care, finding jobs and houses, and encouraging people to take part in sports and education. The Kibera Integrated Community Self-Help Programme (KICOSHEP) provides care and advice for people with HIV/AIDS. They also have a youth centre

where youngsters like Beatrice can go for health information and advice. The centre supports orphans and vulnerable children as well as organising sports and social events for young people.

We first met Beatrice at the KICOSHEP primary school, where she later graduated top of her class. In Kibera, most children see education as the best way to escape from the slum.

The Kenyan Government and UN HABITAT have now started building new homes in Kibera so that thousands of people in the slum have better living conditions.

Since this book was written, Beatrice has left Kibera and gone on to study at a girls' boarding school in Nairobi. It looks as though her dream will come true!

Wendy Stone

ONCE UPON A TIME
Niki Daly

Sarie doesn't like school. Every time she has to take out her reading book, her voice disappears and the other children tease her. But one person understands how she feels – Ou Missus, an old lady living across the veld, who tells wonderful stories. . .

HERD BOY
Niki Daly

Malusi is a herd boy, tending to his grandfather's sheep and goats among the mountains. Can he save his lambs from the hungry baboon stalking the flock? And who is the old man in the shiny car who encourages the boy in his dream of being President? This beautiful picture book, set in rural South Africa, is about a boy who dares to dream of a big future. It is a story of empowerment, self-belief and leadership, inspired by the life of former President Nelson Mandela.

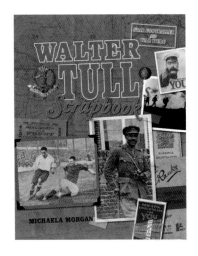

WALTER TULL'S SCRAPBOOK
Michaela Morgan

Walter Tull is a hero of our time. The grandson of a slave and raised in an orphanage, he was one of Tottenham Hotspurs' star players and later became the first black officer in the British Army. His bravery and leadership in the trenches of the First World War won him a recommendation for the Military Cross. Insulted on the pitch because of his colour, he achieved recognition at a time when black footballers were virtually unknown and military law stopped non-Europeans from becoming officers. *Walter Tull's Scrapbook* traces his eventful life in words and pictures and, using newly published photographs, takes a fresh look at a truly remarkable man.

Frances Lincoln titles are available from all good bookshops.
You can also buy books and find out more about your favourite titles, authors and illustrators on our website: www.franceslincoln.com